P9-DMS-826

COLLECTED POEMS

ED COX

Cox, Ed, (1946-1992)

Poems in this volume originally appeared in Calvert Review, December, Diana's Bi-Monthly, Fag Rag, Gargoyle, Gay People's News, Gay Sunshine, Hanging Loose, Interchange, Mass Transit, Painted Bride Quarterly, Pellet, Phoebe, Salt Lick, Sewanee Review, Takoma, the Washington Post, Washington Review, Washout Quarterly, and Writer's Digest, and in the anthologies: Angels of the Lyre, none of the above, and Orgasms of Light.

Copyright 2001 by Laura Cox Lunsford
All rights reserved
Printed in the United States of America

First Edition

ISBN: 0-931181-10-0

Special thanks to Winston Leyland of Gay Sunshine Press who gave this project his blessing and allowed us to reprint Ed's poems from *Waking*. Completists in search of the First Edition should take note that *Waking* is still in print and copies may be obtained from Gay Sunshine Press, P.O. Box 410690, San Francisco, CA 94141 or www.gaysunshine.com

Every effort has been made to locate the photographers who snapped the cover photo and the Cairo Hotel rooftop photo on p.83 for permission to print their work. We hope they'll contact us so we can offer our appreciation.

Paycock Press
3819 No. 13th Street · Arlington, VA 22201

Introduction

These are the words of a poet who has a keen eye for the beauty and
power of the ordinary, an ear open to the plain talk of a mother and her
child, of folks sitting in a cafeteria, or of an anxious patient, trying to alert
anyone and everyone to what might well be seriously wrong. These are the
words, too, of a sensitive, introspective person who has no interest in
showing off, no inclination for the exaggerations and distortions which a
way with language can tempt a writer to offer the reader. Not least, these
are the words of someone who has known loneliness and moments of
sadness; who has stumbled with hurt and confusion; who is still searching
his soul, trying to find a direction for himself in this life.

I have been reading Ed Cox's poems for years—one, then another, and by
now his way with words is delightfully familiar: the voice of a man who
reaches out to others, especially those who are in trouble, who are having
a hard time of it for one or another reason. Some of my students, shown
his poems, remark upon the unselfconscious nature of his gentleness, his
compassion, which is directed not at the manipulation of abstractions, but
at particular men, women, children or at any venerable part of this world
of nature. Here is someone who lives well outside the academy, who has no
acquaintances with corridors of power and money, whose statements are
tentative, qualified, observant of others rather than dedicated to himself.
He sings of small children with few prospects, of the elderly, soon enough
to leave us, and in hard circumstances during those last months or longer.
He sings of those small moments in apparently inconsequential lives—
another District of Columbia than the one of fat-cat lobbyists and windbag
politicians and state dinners attended by the smug, the arrogant, the utterly
self-important. His music has to do with life's little ironies, with the earnest
and honest efforts of unpretentious folk to catch their breaths, to get
through one day, then the next. These are people who don't follow the
Dow Jones or have the ear of law-makers or executives who run
companies, or indeed, America itself. They are people who attend one
another, out of desperation and love both; and who have other things to
do than sit waiting for reporters to come with fawning awe or clever
provocations.

"I love walking down a plain street where plain folks are doing their
living," I once heard William Carlos Williams say—intent on a severe
reprimand to lots of fancy folks in fancy neighborhoods living their
throughly fancy lives. In the shadow of Washington's monuments and
town-houses and extravagant restaurants Ed Cox has shared Dr. Williams'
love of the plain—sung to it, helping bring its various wonders to us, and
thereby helped redeem it, not to mention us.

— Robert Coles

Publisher's Note

Ed Cox was a living breathing part of Washington literary life and lore. His early death in 1992 before publication of his magnum opus, *Part of*, was tragedy on a grand scale. I'm glad to be part of this project to right that wrong, glad to play catalyst for Ed's family and friends (a galaxy of immeasurable proportions).

What originally began as a plan to publish *Part of* rapidly evolved into a volume of Collected Poems. (Note that I don't say Complete Poems. Ed gave untold numbers of poems to people. And there are more scattered throughout his numerous journals.) This volume reprints Ed's two rare out of print chapbooks, includes the long poem about his parents, and finally puts the unpublished manuscript he spent so many years assembling into print. In addition, we've added one last poem as a coda of sorts. It's meant to be a surprise, like an unlisted track at the end of a compact disc.

There is some repetition in the poems. By running the chapbooks in their entirety, a couple reappear in various guises throughout the collection. I thought it was worthwhile to see how Ed revised some of his poems from book to book: "After the Beat," "Seeing," and "Waiting" for example. I found it particularly insightful that the "We" in the earlier versions of "Waiting" became an "I" in the final version. A few other unrevised poems are duplications as well, but it seemed right to Bob Lunsford (who handled the layout) and myself to run the chapbooks as they were. If that meant a little repetition, okay then. We hope you understand our desire to be true to the original chapbooks. I think the reader will also note that the poem "Ezra and Agnes" taken from the chapbook *Blocks* was the seed toward the longer more involved "These Two", and that the "Part Of" in *Waking* is perhaps a genesis for the cycle that grew into the book *Part of*. At least that's how it seems to me on a rainy June night.

I think readers are hungry for the human spirituality Ed offers in these poems. I hope so. It's nice to see them in print, nice to have a book of Ed's heartfelt memories and dreams to pass on to a friend, nice to see the book nestled on the shelf between Jayne Cortez and Robert Creeley. I hope you agree.

—Richard Peabody

Contents

Blocks

Waiting   3
First Day   4
This Morning   5
Getting Back There   6
After the Rent   7
Family Album   8
My Aunt   9
Years Later   10
First Hunt   11
Listening   12
I Want to Tell Them   13
It Happens This Way   14
Evening News   15
Anticipation   16
Poem   20
Letter to Brother Andrew   21
All These Thin Lines   22
Jamie   23
Harvard Graduate   24
    Speaking to His Troops
Ezra and Agnes   25
Rain   26

Waking

Windows   31

What Do I Know   32

Seeing   33

Third Quarter   34

Basketball   35

Innocence   36

High School   37

Hitchhiking   38

Waiting   39

Room   40

Cruising   41

Three in the Morning   42

Light   43

face   44

Anticipation   45

Dupont Circle   49

Evening   50

Faggot   51

Poem For Hart Crane   52

Sunrise   54

garden   55

From the City   56

Part of   57

Sleep   58

Waking   59

dreamed was in room   60

Companion   61

This Morning   62

Seed

Remember   69

These Two:
  Ezra and Agnes   73

Part of

I   Beginning   85
At Dawn   87
Seeing   88
After the Rent   89
To My Brother Lost   90
The Faith   91
Together   92
Family   93
Names   94
Passing It On   95

II   Each Other   97
One   99
Waiting   100
Search   101
Bulbs Live On   102
Departure   103
Entwined   104
Cuddle the Bricks   105
Passenger   106

III   Common Good   107
Her Recounting   109
Benediction   110
Throughout the Day   111
The Wanderer   112
These Clouds   113
Testimonies   114
The Test   115

The Trapped Whales   117
Mary in November   118
On the Lake   119

IV   This Realm   121
Harvard Graduate Speaking to His Troops   123
First Hunt   124
In the Before   125
Three in the Morning   126
At the Fountain   127
The Other Side   128
Medical Report   129
Shells of Milk Cartons   130
The Secret Lives of Animals   131
Carnegie Library, Park Bathroom   132
Broken is the Cup   133

V   Part of   135
The Moons of Mars   137
Last Light   138
Note for the Fireplace   139
The Composer   140
Your Realm   141
The Vulnerable   142
At the Edge   143
Voices   144
Moving   145
The Work Sweater   146
Part of   147

The Dream of a Companion   152

Blocks

Blocks

was originally published in an edition of 500 copies by
Some of Us Press   1972
Washington, D.C.

Love and thanks to Rudd Fleming, Josephine Jacobsen,
Lee Lally and Michael Lally for their support and
encouragement.

"One of the things that is a very important thing to know
is how you are feeling inside to the words that are coming
out to be outside you."

o Gertrude Stein

Waiting

I've no idea, sense of place,
where you might be when you stare out
across this crowded bar. Your eyes
have found some space I can not see:
rooms you've slept in, long streets,
the face of a man you've met here before.

You keep your head down, look up only
when the sound of the door opens
or closes over the song someone has played
three times. In ten minutes
you've pulled the blue plaid cuff
of your shirt sleeve twice to check the time.
It's late. I could tell you that.

We wait, stall for this person
we believe—tell ourselves,
write in letters to distant friends,—
will walk in, sit down, and turning
hear the words we find in our hands.

First Day

I'm walking to school—St. Joseph's—1952. I'm wearing a plaid shirt
and one of my father's large neckties. It's red and has all kinds of
bright colored triangles.   Two blocks from Stanton Park,
a block past Lee's Cat & Dog Hospital, I can see Union Station. It's
a large gray building.   I cross the intersection. Streetcar
tracks still wet. Curb falling apart in one place. I notice the small,
round stones on the underside of concrete.   I'm a block from
school. Other children are also walking to school. Some with their
mothers or fathers. Some alone. A girl, about ten, is carrying a brown
paper bag with a doughnut printed blue on it. A boy my own age is
sitting on black iron steps over a Chinese laundry. Thin white curtains
in the window.   A man is getting into his car. He's wearing
a brown hat. Another man is wearing a black hat. One boy is chasing
another boy. I'm thinking about my shoes. The right one has a hole
in it. But my mother put a cardboard backing from one of my father's
shirts inside the shoe. It's ok.   My little sister, Laura Anne, is
at home. She has blond hair. I have blond hair.   I can hear
the voices of children in the schoolyard. The schoolyard is surrounded
by large walls. Children are playing dodge ball. One small boy is
crying. A nun has her arms around him. Her black dress covers her
shoes.   I walk up the steps to the playground. I go to the
wall and watch the dodge ball game.   Some girls, too, are
playing hop-scotch. They're tossing things at the numbered squares.
One girl tosses a key with string on it.   I can see pigeons on top
of the rectory. There are some pieces of coal near the door at the
back of the rectory.   The bell rings. Everyone is running to
line up in front of one of the nuns. I run too. I'm a first-grader. I
get in the first-grader line. The nun for the first grade tells us to follow
her and she clicks a wood thing that's in her hand. She has a smooth
face.   We walk to the door. She stands in front of it and
presses a finger to her lips. We stop talking. She opens the door. She
tells us all to quietly take a seat. I take one. A girl takes the seat next
to me. We all sit down. I can hear the door shut.   I think of my
mother, how many blocks it is to my house—the one with the tree
my father says grows green cigars people get sick from when they smoke
them. Everything is so quiet. I want to go to the park with my mother
and watch the cars go around the circle.

4

This Morning

for Stanley

The river, Potomac, wider
stretching calm

sky for the third day
so vast and clear

and you driving
anticipating lights

sudden stops
turning once to ask

how near are we
to where we're going

Getting Back There

for Michael Lally

1.

We were driving north
New York   signs with Dutch names
places you would talk us back to:

streets, wheeling through Holland Tunnel
(the other one I can't remember)
drunk   high school punk   as you put it
off for a night

                  where did you stand?
                  what corners?

when the doors opened, when those people
stepped out of the late fifties
you could hear notes

sounds of words from piano and saxophone
and I bet your hands touched,
you touched them
pulled at your blue Banlon shirt
stood there, waiting, probably alone

2.

The boy at Peoples' Drugstore:
fourteen, following me around
through the magazines but no bananas
to be seen   He wanted me to look back
say, "Hello, what are you doing?"

3.

I want to talk to people again
like I used to. Not afraid.
Say hello to them.
Go up and tell them how very important
it is for us to look up once in a great while,
give in some, admit that it's really good
to be living,
that there's a way of getting back there.

6

After the Rent

On payday, after the rent
and checking off of other cares,
Dad would bring mother
a box of Schrafft's assorted candy
or flowers coned in his right hand—
the wrapping paper thin,
vulnerable as the orphan
in the sheer brown of his eyes.

Wordless, nearing thirty-four,
He'd stand before her
like a small boy
watching the Richmond sky clear
for the first time, saying:
"Mama, these are for you."

Family Album

1.

Two men standing beside a black Ford. 1921. A woman, young, seated on the running board, has her head bowed to the ground. In the distance, to the left, the roof of a barn.

2.

A heavy-set woman looks out from the top of a small, arched bridge. Her hair is tied back, gray. She is Grandmother O'Flynn. The neck of her dress has a white collar.

3.

Communion procession. A priest is looking at one of the boys who is out of the picture. The door, main door of St. James' Church, is open.

4.

Front porch with a bench swing suspended to the right of the doorway. A large black cat is walking in some flowers. Top right of the photograph is torn.

5.

My cousin Ed. He's wearing an army uniform. Two medals.

6.

Atlantic City: the 20's. Lots of people on the boardwalk. Men wearing straw hats. There's a breeze. All the flags are ruffled.

7.

My Uncle Dan. Seated, legs crossed. He's smoking and holds the cigarette in his left hand.

8.

Badly faded, brown. People are waving.

My Aunt

My Aunt Mary,
steeped in the Blessed Virgin,
brewed tea twice from the same bag;
hanging them in the kitchen window
while the war raged across Europe.
Pictures of her uniformed sons
and a small choir of nephews
stationed the cross in every room.

Religious,
she worked at the Old Shrine store—
dusting the Infant of Prague
during slack hours.

Years Later

They're burning a village.
Men move about with machine
metal boxes they open
in the faces of children.

There are planes and long islands
that stretch below more planes.
They are headed north.
Their large, swift shadows
plow ricefields,
haul the names of women and men,
dropping them from wings—
wings that turn away from us
when the film ends,
projector stops.

First Hunt

I watch the village
through a forest of rice
and wire barbed with teeth
the mud brown of mountain
and junction stream.

A woman, mouth open,
flails words and arms
in the wake
of roar and wing.

I recall the wet breath
of the dying deer
I shot in my fourteenth year.
It was in the fall
in West Virginia.

Listening

It does happen.
We wake to the dark,
the star, the window left open.

The street is empty.
The sky thick and wide
and pressing.

It's there, then,
that we make decisions:
accept pipes
breathing with us,
the names on each breath.

And a dog barks.
Always an animal
sounding back.

There is rock
that would speak
if we listened, eyes.

We can hear each other
before it is all still.

I Want To Tell Them

There is a clot at the back of my head.
I've told them, more than once,
that it's there, has been there
as long as I can remember.

I told them the first night,
I told them last night.
All they do is listen,
send for the doctor.
And he listens, though more attentive,
and he leaves.

I know it. They know it.
There is a clot at the back of my head.
There is flesh, stars, and rooms
that do not appear on the chart
at the far end of my bed.

I'm afraid.
That is all I really want to say.
They know it.

It Happens This Way:

Towards the close of day
an old man will wake
after a long, deep nap.
He'll stay in bed,
watch the window and listen
for the traffic on his street.
Then he'll get up,
unfold his brown pants pants—
adjust frayed suspenders.

There are stairs.
They step down into the kitchen
and out onto the backporch.
There is light there.
Large frames of it that the man
likes to stand in.

When it rains,
when there is that constant sound
over the house, he often crouches,
bends low to press his face
to the smooth grain of the wood floor.
He thinks of the neighbor's children,
birds that fly into tall buildings,
the time his wife—
    for what seemed like an hour—
stood outside their first home.

When he pushed down, when he
made the car sound its
sound, she turned,
walked to the fully packed van
they'd rented and said
she didn't see how people could take it
time and again: the leaving,
the being alone.

Evening News

Summer,   5:30,   Northwest
Washington. Third day
of humid weather.
Stoops lined with young men
and women who drink wine
from brown paper bags,
                sip on Cokes.
Windows open.
Drone of air-conditioners.
Screen doors shut.
Trucks back-fire.

A man, middle-aged,
stares from the second floor
of a yellow brick apartment building.
Behind him, slowly, someone drinks
from a glass of water.
He's thirsty.
That's the sound.

Anticipation

Four and a half hours to go
and I'll be reading this to you.
Right now, where I work, I'm nervous
about being nervous about the word WEAK.

This this way   of using words   HELPS.
Outside the form, the structure of it all.
That has been bothering me:

the need to be "logical" "manly"
"rational"   SANE.
The structure of it, the form of it.

              *   *   *

Dori, woman I work with three days a week,
talked about this. How for years
she saw herself
as a MONSTER.   INHUMAN,
living in a place that turned in on itself:

               man in battle—

               no more dirt.

               no earth to hide in—

wanting to crawl

               inside himself

the word "fetal"
               the way I sleep sometimes
comes to mind:
               how I can begin to tell myself
that it's all right to be a child.

Dori walks back into the office
after the first page.   Reads.   Then:

"never thought of myself as a WOMAN—

               always girl or chick."

We talk.   Nervous.

Afraid I'll be perceived as some kind of fool—

and I'm not that. That turning in AGAIN.

                    *   *   *

Dori, again, comes to mind.

"People need wailing walls"   Jews,

          pogroms,   drawing swastikas,

          age nine,   on sidewalks.

Wailing walls. Sirens return. But no noise.

Red light. Mother. In the kitchen. Ammonia

sliding   wet   tiles look on her face

but no noise—FORGIVE.

                    Just then

sudden spurts   open arms

returning.   SOMETHING LIKE

movies without sound   man standing

on a hill   watching an explosion

fluttering of ash   in flame   but no sound.

Distant, watching   an entire town rain down

LIKE BOMBS.

                    Women and men going around
with fuses in their breath.

                    The girl,
thirteen years old, the psychiatrist Laing

talked about being SCHIZOPHRENIC. She said:
"There is a BOMB inside of ME."

                    *   *   *

Once, watching TV

                    I saw a man throw
himself on the ground

17

—wanting a baby bomb
all inside of HIM.

        Then his body, a huge fish,
flopped-up   off
          the ground   dull thud
scales
      side of blood
            more distant.

       *   *   *

Groups of people do whatever "it" is to me.

I panic,
     turn inside myself.
Seventh grade: afraid to reach out

turn off   the light—

buses   New Metro   showers   in Japan—

lost in the woods   not knowing who

to turn to   because of panic   panic at the thought

of touching another man's body

        even my own—

& I think of priests,

        confession,

     smelling my hands before devotion

        candles,

monasteries: IMAGES   IMAGES

     to hold onto.

        I need that,

the boy at Harper's Ferry

        wandering off:

always in some small group

                    a person

suddenly wounded

                    and amazed—

the way people will walk

                         three blocks

          to feed pigeons

     my father's face   at 68

     strangely   lit

       when I kiss him

       and he doesn't know

       I'm a FAGGOT—

trees,

                    small pools of water

          those asterisks

                    in Michael's poems

like black   perfect snow

that I sometimes know

                         outside all of this

     I believe in myself.

Poem

for Miles, Age 2

I heard a man crying.
He'd been walking on the beach
and found a great whale dying.
It was a slow death.

The man saw the sun
in the whale's one still eye.
He ran to the ocean
and returned with what was left
of a handful of water.
He patted it on the whale's lips.

A small, green-blue fish,
wiggled up to the two of them:
the man, the whale.
He kissed the whale and swam
up over the sand to the man.
The fish said, "I love you"
to the man.

This is why sea shells sound
the way they do.
They've nothing else to say.

Letter to Brother Andrew

Today, in the small field behind the pottery house,
the milk pods were open; their mouths fluff white and full
as those of the now three grazing cows.

Many changes since my last letter—
milk, and the bridge has been repaired.

And my penmanship, with slow grace,
as you can see, has improved somewhat.
Notice how the swirl of the e's
trace the pages like undotted eyes.
But that, my dear brother, is too much of me—
forgive this wandering; this talk of myself.

Brother George, I am sad I must write,
is in bad spirits. Since we found him
weeping in the garden, searching for the key
to the wine cellar,
his words have had no good phrase to say.
Late at night, even on St. Augustine's Day.
he curses and damns us all.

Last night at supper I thought of you,
your quiet face, eyes closed,
listening to the rule of order read.
And I might add, in I hope a fair note,
that Brother Matthew is reading again—
though the light pitch of his voice at serving
could use the reach of our humble prayers.

I will bring this to a close.
For I hear movement,
our brothers readying for worship.

When I pass your room
I often stand at the open door—
watching the light fold a sheet on your bare bed;
the dawn a pillow where you would rest your head.

Andrew, why do I miss you so much?

All These Thin Lines

for my brother, Jimmy

You're off again with your friends
and it's three in the morning.
In the sketch you named "Resistance",
scotch-taped to the livingroom wall,
David kneels, hands clasped,
staring at the dove your charcoals tamed.
The lines of his black eyes as pure
as the way you often say by phone,
when you're away, I'm alone,
"Ed, I love you. "

You're fifteen.
Your eyes lure me back to that time
when I watched you sleep—
whisper in the night the names
of your dreams. You were six then.
You moaned, quivered after kicking
back all of those covers.

It happens that way, Jimmy.
Everyday you're off again
and me and your friends and mine:
being born, sleeping, dreaming,
drawing from the dark one more day.

Jamie

Oh, I'm afraid of the dark. I'm afraid of it. I'm afraid of the window. I'm afraid that there's someone behind the door. I feel sick. I feel hungry. I feel that maybe my mother and father don't love me. I'm afraid I'll die. I'm afraid of fists, dogs in the street. They might bite me. When the television goes off, when all the dark moves into that small dot, I get afraid. Flowers get sick. Cats die from poison. I don't want people to leave me.

Harvard Graduate Speaking
to His Troops

It is important to be approximate.
Maintain a steady hand.
Your eyes should hold the enemy—
    like a small vessel at offertory.
But don't prolong the process.
Too much contemplation,
    a philosophy teacher once confided to me,
    distorts the image.
That is, you begin to think, to dwell:
    dreams and music can stir across
    another man's face if you stall.
Immediacy, then, is the crucial word:
    our primary objective.

Be true to your weapon.
One has to be true to something.

Ezra and Agnes

1.

There were times then
in those days when
my father vomited at night
   staggering like a man
   shot through the head
   in the prime of his life
that fear was something
I crayoned the clowns
that filled my Saturday mornings
when only I saw light breathe
in the early hours.

Television later showed me why
Danny Thomas was the kind of man
I wanted to go fishing with
when I stood at the bedroom window.

Twenty-six and I count this pain
by the leaves each fall, spring rain,
winter when rocks touch
like imagined dead cowboys must
and summers of dry, thirsty clay.

No matter how I balance them
I always end up loving him.

2.

My mother wakes near midnight.
Cautious at fifty-nine,
she braces every step when she turns
to the bathroom.

Time passes and she walks out
holding her stomach, asking:
"Have you ever had diarrhea?"

Rain

for my parents

Rain don't go away.
I'm alone on Friday night,
restless,
into counting faults.

I've made phone calls
visits to friends
my sister
my mother who only lives in
Bladensburg, Maryland:

She might be up
listening to you
wondering
how she has gotten
this far—

almost sixty years
listening to rain:
evicted twice
in the snow

she likes windows
has always sat by them.
I like windows.

I get up
to use the bathroom,
make tea.
I hear you.

There are so many ways
of saying so many things.
I'm not the first person
to listen to you,
to talk to you.

People talk to walls,
people who aren't there,
themselves,
dogs that come in
out of a storm, wet,
waiting for a big towel
to dry them off.

So many people alone.
No one to talk to them.
Rain, that's what you do.

Snow is white,
wants to be seen
hardly heard.
Wind makes other things
     trees
     long hallways
give up their sounds.
Rain, you talk back to us.
We listen.

Even a squirrel.
Squirrel that is injured,
making sounds
that hurt in its eyes—
left paw cupped.

You move mountains,
generators,
whole villages, leaves
inside a child's eyes
so that he'll get up
     find his way
     through the dark
to mother or
father's room.

Sometimes the parent
just doesn't know.
Maybe because the child
can't speak yet.
That's when they listen.

Rain, you teach us
the things we're always trying
to learn.
Things that for so long
confused me
about almost everything:
Algebra,
the way some people look
    so desperate,
    why people die
    hurt—
women in the films
that cry over something small,
infant.

The way you fall tonight
maybe tomorrow
    five years from now,
    ten,
just the way you fall
but get up
giving life to all of us.

Waking

Waking
was originally published in an edition of 1000 copies by
Gay Sunshine Press   June 1977
San Francisco

"We are made of words. They are our
only reality, or at least, the only testi-
mony of our reality."

o Octavio Paz

Windows

wake to rain
breathing of friend   Bobbie
his head   brown hair

wanting him to move
push away covers
to cock   legs
I wanted to touch
while he was in sleep

me shaking   erect,
moon   leaf
smell of his body

wanting him to stir
                        slow
afraid as me to touch
be together in dark
through walls
door shutting
two flights up

What Do I Know

except I'm fifteen
like moments of quiet
that come in the morning
and know I can't tell my parents
how I feel inside
when I visit my best friend

we spend the night together
at his Mom's apartment
on weekends and play cards   chess
or watch television

last weekend we got caught
in the rain when we went camping
near the woods where the trains
change tracks

when we were at the bottom of the hill
the thunder started
                    we ran
as fast as we could   reaching
for the small trees that grow there
and half way up the rain came down
and my friend started to laugh out loud
and we were wet with clay that was red
and kind of orange

we took off our clothes
hung them from the pole that held
the tent up
              fell to sleep
in the same sleeping bag

what do I know but that I want
to tell you this
how good it feels to touch
be touched

Seeing

Through microscope when I was nine.
Taking cork top off bottle
of shrimp eggs, tapping so few would fall
to water on slide.

Placing under metal grips
which if bent back too much would break off.
Saying to myself: I can do this,
I can close my left eye
without using my hand.

Seeing with right eye a blur
and adjusting two knobs
two circles became one
where still eggs were.

I wanted some thing to push out
from inside and swim free.

Third Quarter

50-45 and your coach
calls time out   you stand
by bench
          shake head
          sweat hair
                    cling
                    to you

there's water
to drink
          towel that hangs
          around neck shoulders
          on chest

Basketball

for Tim Dlugos

two boys jump from lines under net
one boy's right hand reaches
arm extends to let ball touch backboard
fall black hair evening
sky over Georgetown
brilliant in their leaping

Innocence

we'd end up going home after school
wondering how it was we killed baby Jesus
who later died on the cross
and was kind to the thieves who died with him

they told us about the sin of touching
yourself   that you didn't let the white stuff
come out of you all on your own

the tongue was to stay inside
not to reach outside   you shouldn't see tunnels
or assholes or visualize a wet mouth
or head of cock growing out of underwear
checking to make sure all there

you couldn't have this   you did that
you   ever since birth   were responsible
for the sins of the world   carried around
inside of you something
that had to be in control

they didn't want to see   know about
altar boys who stayed up all night
watching the Saturday late movie   going to bed
with butter on their lips   fourteen year old
bodies full with basketball movement
waiting to touch
after so many hours
sleeping together

High School

Table, wallet, change.   Window.   Waking to room and book
near side of bed, alarm clock.   Downstairs door opens,
someone enters house.   Sunday.   Most of boarders away

Last night.   Going to bar off Thomas Circle.   Go to
sandwich shop after leaving.   Coffee.   Stand near window,
look out.   Man walks by and looks in, looks at me.   I look
back.   He keeps walking and turns his head. Stops,
continues to look and then walks on.

I go home. Remember high school yearbook in room.   Photograph
of football players in shower.   Base of stomach upwards.
Thin lines of hair.   One boy with nipples that stood out,
circular, erect tip.   Right arm over shoulder of another boy.
Wet.   Head tilted back to side.   Imagine going to locker room
and man sitting next to locker touching nipples.   Him
standing to dry off and pulling towel between legs.   Holding
soft towel over head and staring at me, gently twisting right
hand around and standing erect and looking down between lockers
to see if anyone there.   Wrapping towel around waist.   Turning
to me. Walking over, sitting down.

Hitchhiking

on Massachusetts Avenue   19   just off work
stand   right foot on grass near curb   tree
hand in pocket   pull zipper half way down

cars   station wagons   cabs
pick-up trucks   bus   van

eyes of drivers   open door   glance
at arms   crotch before see face
positioning myself once on New Jersey Turnpike
ride from boy my own age had sex   toll card
dashboard light

later I asked
if he thought I was homosexual
he said he didn't know

Waiting

I've no idea, sense of place,
where you might be when you stare out
across this crowded bar.   Your eyes
have found some space I can't see:
rooms you've slept in, long streets,
face of a man you've met here before.

You keep your head down, look up only
when the sound of the door opens
or closes over the song someone has played
three times. In ten minutes
you've pulled the blue plaid cuff
of your shirt sleeve twice to check the time.
It's late.   I could tell you that.

We wait, stall for this person
we believe—tell ourselves,
write in letters to distant friends—
will walk in, sit down, and turning
hear the words we find in our hands.

Room

we got to after get out of car
walk up stairs
when we sit   fall

blood goes to where it will then
veins arms   legs
body inside   curves
places wet

Cruising

someone will come up

approach you on street

and say

I haven't been here long

this place   this way

this wind   these windows

Three in the Morning

Stillness thick.
Dark covers door,   corner,
walls,   paintings without face.

Awake while others sleep.

This is time,
moment only you share,
when unbutton shirt
touch chest—
hand an earth in itself
moving sure,   slow.

Light rises between fingers.

Light

in room   covers around
morning   7 o'clock
get out of bed   take shower   cold
back in bed   body warm
close   hands touch
small fire
to begin day

face

warm

chests

suction

turn

leap

thick

swallow

hold

hair

edge

of

mattress

mouth

on

neck

fuse

Anticipation

Four and a half hours to go
and I'll be reading this to you.
Right now, where I work, I'm nervous
about being nervous about the word WEAK.

This   this way   of using words   HELPS
outside the form, the structure of it all.
That has been bothering me:

the need to be "logical"   "manly"
"rational"   SANE.
The structure of it, the form of it.

             *   *   *

Dori, woman I work with three days a week,
talked about this. How for years
she saw herself
as a MONSTER,   INHUMAN,
living in a place that turned in on itself:

      man in battle—

      no more dirt.

      no earth to hide in—

wanting to crawl

      inside himself
the word "fetal"

               the way I sleep sometimes
comes to mind:
             how I can begin to tell myself
that it's all right to be a child.

Dori walks back into the office
after the first page.   Reads.   Then:
"never thought of myself as a WOMAN—
             always girl or chick."

We talk.   Nervous.

Afraid I'll be perceived as some kind of fool—

and I'm not that.   That turning in AGAIN.

                    *   *   *

Dori, again, comes to mind.

"People need wailing walls"   Jews,

            pogroms,   drawing swastikas,

            age nine,   on sidewalks.

Wailing walls.   Sirens return.   But no noise.

Red light.   Mother.   In the kitchen.   Ammonia

sliding   wet tiles   look on her face

but no noise—FORGIVE

                Just then

sudden spurts   open arms

returning.   SOMETHING LIKE

movies without sound   man standing

on a hill   watching an explosion

fluttering of ash   in flame   but no sound.

Distant, watching   an entire town rain down

LIKE BOMBS.

                Women and men going around

with fuses in their breath.

                The girl

thirteen years old, the psychiatrist Laing

talked about being SCHIZOPHRENIC. She said:

"There is a BOMB inside of ME."

*　　*　　*

Once, watching TV
          I saw a man throw
himself on the ground
      —wanting a baby bomb
all inside of HIM.
         Then his body, a huge fish,
flopped-up off
        the ground   dull thud
scales
     side of blood
         more distant.

*　　*　　*

Groups of people do whatever "it" is to me.

I panic,
     turn inside myself.
Seventh grade: afraid to reach out
turn off   the light—

buses   New Metro   showers   in Japan—
lost in the woods   not knowing who
to turn to   because of panic   panic at the thought
of touching another man's body
        even my own—
& I think of priests,
     confession,
  smelling my hands before devotion
     candles,
monasteries: IMAGES   IMAGES
  to hold onto.
        I need that,

the boy at Harper's Ferry
         wandering off:
always in some small group
        a person
suddenly wounded
     and amazed—

47

the way people will walk
                    three blocks
        to feed pigeons
my father's face at   68
    strangely lit
        when I kiss him
            and he doesn't know
                I'm a FAGGOT—
trees,
            small pools of water
        those asterisks
            in Michael's poems
like black   perfect snow
that I sometimes know
            outside all of this
I believe in myself.

Dupont Circle

curve of wooden bench   except for entrance
places where people enter   go

                    two drinking
                    fountains
across street, urinals: men,   women

              watch men go there
              remember bar
              man looking out
              under table legs hands
              to touch someone

basement hallway   corner where pipes were
you could sit up on them

                  sleeping   18
                  not being asleep
masturbating in bathroom
after friend's hand on leg in Navy
because couldn't go to where he wanted to go

:faggot   sissy   lame-punk   queer   cocksucker   queen
mama's boy   little girl   fairy

quiet of morning   early morning
pulling arm from underneath him
to waking and move body against

                          fall asleep again
in dream call out to another man

Evening

a Mustang pulls up in alley   two young men   one of
them gets out of car to go into rear entrance
of house   other stays behind driver's wheel   he looks
up to window where I look from   he stretches as in
waking from sleep   leans over to see if friend
is returning   looks back up and stretches again   rears
up in seat and unbuttons shirt to belt   it's dark but
light from building through window touches on him   he rubs
chest   mouths right hand and spits into   leans back
up into seat and unbuckles belt   left hand hidden but
left shoulder moves slow   he leans up into seat for
moment left hand tight around through windowshield light
pulling

Faggot

torch

bundle of wood

placed at feet

men stare out

in disbelief

Poem for Hart Crane

1–

All night the river draws tight.
The Bridge looms wide,
                              green steel,
Brackish,
         the cords drawn to ice,
Breath inching,
    pushing out at all sides.

2–

This would be a place
Where you would walk,   dark,
No cadence,
No climbing rush to trains,
In a cord of place
That brings towns,   early hours,
Strolls home,
Those quick cruises to the docks.

All here,   the green rising.
Stretched out over the River.
Bridge, you.
Light off the Coast of Mexico:
Lost cord,   Phrase
And you a poem,   Always.

3–

What is to be learned from you?
The Twenties.   Names of presidents
I don't care to remember, recall,
Out of text their prohibitions
Driving you to riskier bars
Where men
              if an eye flash
Stood out   cords on a Bridge   a gap.

52

That Bridge as wide in your room
As your words trafficking back and forth:
Train, Bridge, your name—
                    the constant
                    traveller—
The lone walk: Bar, Bridge, and Ships.

You: engulfed
Afraid as all of us.

Sunrise
for Dave

in room   outside on roof rain
beginning of day and waking remember
how colors look from one side of room
and differently when you go up to them

brown   something rising
above lines of green
water in sky where is blue
and on canvas what is inside comes out

someone throws bread from window
ice makes sound   small birds walk on
in morning   even if rain   snow coming down
there's always sun
warmth coming up somewhere

garden

mouth

over

tulip

lips

touch

stem

pollen

river

bikers

hair

back

near

water

From the City

for Tim Corbett

we learned movement of hands
to hips
             ballet of street words
hanging out on corners
in December   became refined
in our eating habits
                        held potato chip
well above head
                     cupped cigarette
in school hall
                  found aristocracy in faces
of workers—fathers, brothers—
returning from work
                     came to know
the class distinction of Chuck Taylor
tennis shoes
                  the absolutely fine attraction
of bodies in summer,
                         tank tops   legs apart
inviting us to stand upright
against police cars   big wheels
from the suburbs

Child, we were coming out
long before we knew it!

Part of

One morning returned from sleep to rain.   Attic above
room gave comforting sound.   Steady falling.   Dream
still with me.   Was walking beside creek, could see
many arms of grass near edge moving.   Was trying to
say hello to person on other side.   Being here.

Stayed in bed.   Stayed with sound.   Covers, folding
pillow, turning on side to look out window.   Rain,
my breathing, constant sound within, above house.
Remember going on hike when 13 and valley as quilt.
Brown, green, yellow, small stream lines across land.
Silo.   Being here.

My mother said she came every day for two weeks to visit
me at hospital.   On bus.   Making circle to look out
from.   Holy card.   Purse.   Metal box in church, coin,
candles like terrace farming in geography book.   Being here.

He said you learn to look at all these things.   You
can't turn away.   Even when hurts.   You're quilt ground.
Patience of different colors given to cloth in metal
hoops by needle.   Wet thread with tongue to go through.
Mouth dry when wake from dream.   Pull covers close.
Sheets.   Soft against face.   Being here.

Sleep

for Steve

we do what we have to

pull out little thing
at rear of clock

remember rain   light
through window
when seven

in bed   be still
close eyes   listen
to breathing

wake and world
returns again

wonder   leaf
small animal drinking water
way people stare
across park   in elevator
on street

quiet   thankful
we're here again

Waking

could feel breath
on neck   stiffness
at side   pull you slowly
to face   your cock
close to lips   not touching
mouth soft   round onto you
vein of underside
in throat slowly   mouth wet
slowly pushing into my mouth
again motion wet
hands hold your ass slowly
tight cock in throat wet
pulling you from me   small
opening close to mouth not touching
hand   length   motion
of hands to you   pulling motion
in hand you bend head back
upright   slowly you bend back
in motion   to let go so close
to my lips not touching
your breathing becoming other sound
hand   hair   face   sleep comes
from inside   comes fast
from inside of you   out onto
face   my face is warm
gasp for air   mouth wet
taste of sky   we were biking
along canal   there were clusters
of rock   in river   of morning   of you
now on my face   clear   wide sky

how we can give to each other

dreamed was in room
of concrete
no windows   control panel
at base of wall
and if could understand
controls I wouldn't drown

only person
inside gymnasium leaping
to touch backboard
snap of towels
in large space

young deer   chased
I ran between cars
beam of head lights

ran by ocean
where man held shell

Companion

1–

Walk across school yard.
You're crouched over circle,
move marble,
rub back, forward
with both hands.

2–

Punt football in field
near Anacostia Naval Base.
Two sailors stand by river.
One points to ship on other side.

This Morning

for Stanley

The river, Potomac, wider
stretching calm

sky for third day
so vast and clear

and you driving
anticipating lights

sudden stops
turning once to ask

how near are we
to where we're going

in the rain

here in the park

* *

ivy

under

fingernails

tremor of his hand

* *

candle

moon

on other side

as small boys

we were told

for fire rub sticks

together

cocks

just

touching

sleep

exhausted

dream

open

window

walk

how from your hands

did this come

where in your eyes

did words gather

your mouth holding them

Remember

Everything gone.   Walls as they were.   Windowsill
and paint chipped from openings, closing.   Where plants
were and walking in room alone in quiet of day
beginning.   Sitting there, waiting for coffee to brew.
Leaf on floor.   Thin roots in glass jar from cuttings.
Windowsill and nun in grade school telling story of how
she put seeds outside window and next day they looked
like something from pond.   His sitting by window,
on floor in darkness touching face.   Bending backward,
hands brace floor in head toward hair on neck.   Hair.
Quiet room.   Watching him.   Each one of us different
he said.   Your small wrists as different as hair turning
gray.   Leaving once and park was empty and by fountain
understanding how it is when you listen inside there's
who you are outside of what returns as pain or questions
and not knowing what to do.   The water.   Traffic before
light. Him telling me to let go.   Each of us has been
hurt in some way.

Strength came from understanding.   Silence of being
in room and letting each other into eyes, places would
imagine taking other person or going to with them
to where they'd been.

These Two:

Ezra and Agnes

Dedicated to Rudd Fleming

"May the blessing of light be upon you,
light without and light within."

    o Gaelic Blessing

published in *The Washington Review*
in Oct-Nov 1989

He said the large open windows and few small fans did little to
move the air.

           I was hung-over, sick as a dog. The linotype
           machine squirrted lead. We'd gone to the race track
           in New Jersey, drank all the way back to Union
           Station.

                At seven years the Baptist orphanage. His
father dead, the year before, of tuberculosis.

                          She had to put me
there and she worked long hours in the factory sewing overalls.
We'd sit at the table and just eat molasses and string beans
while the fat matron ate full plates of ham and beans.

                             There's
the story he told about being beneath the weighed down branches
of apple trees. There was a farm, dairy and his apprenticeship
to become a printer.

                Boy, I could throw a baseball, had a curve.
Played shortstop, too.

                The sky is a specked blue map of stars. My
mother waits in the car on a road in West Virginia where they
drove down to buy moonshine. I thought I'd pee myself with all
those dogs barking, she said.

                  I'll tell you, Churchill didn't
give up. The Germans bombed London day and night.

                           Dad was just
eighteen, lanky, all skin and bone. The recruiting officer told
him to go to the nearby market and eat as many bananas, drink all
the water he could hold. He eked, sucked in, held the air,
stepped on the scale, a pound over, into the U.S. Navy.

                             She was a
beauty, pure class. I met her in Shanghai. She was the daughter
of the Spanish ambassador. We went to the best of places. Lots
of Russians and English in the nightclubs. She gave me a silver
tiepin before the fleet sailed.

                That he was a woman's man, he
always said. There was the teacher in New York City he endeared
with his way with words, a song after several drinks. (And that
winter in Chicago, at the *Tribune*, when I got stinking drunk
playing poker,

           met this woman in some hotel bar
           and didn't leave the bed for two

days. My cock was rubbed raw
and she kept asking for more.)
                                        Listen to me:
there's a fucking rat at the foot of the bed and some snakes
crawling in the springs. You damn well better bring me the other
bottle.
          Sprawled sleep of burnt sheets, dark snail-ashen shadows
at the side of the bed where he slept. A stiff belt or two still
in the quart.
                    In high school I'd wait-up past midnight for him to
return from the lobster shift at *The Washington Post,*
                                        long hours
at the keyboard, meeting press deadlines. He'd stop along New
York Avenue
                    for a cup of coffee and a doughnut,
                    buy another dozen to take home.
                                        Often he'd bring
the latest edition of the newspaper and sometimes would talk of
work,
          tell a story about having to take copy
          to a young reporter on the fifth floor—
          note the ellipses
          in the lead paragraph were not proper.
                                        He's seated in a
          rickshaw with a buddy and stares directly at
          the camera. All those curls in his hair,
mother said,
          and he was so handsome.
                              She was the 13th
of sixteen children. Her mother, my grandmother Flynn, stands in
the middle of a small arched bridge
                              in the photograph taken at a
          resort town on the Maryland coast. In England she worked as
          a maid for a wealthy Protestant family, saved her earnings
          for the passage to America.
                              All those who left, made journey
          to the great promises of Columbia. The blight of potatoes,
          stories of those whose hunger made them desperate enough to
          eat the spoiled white meat.
                              You're too young to remember, she
said, the time your red-haired cousins danced at the wedding.

The men let you sip the foam off their beers.

There is this being

at peace in the rain, asphalt of damp mornings.

O Danny Boy,

O Danny Boy, she sang on St. Patrick's Day and cried, talked
about her mother,

how the woman suffered through those last years
and her arms bruised from injections.

He said a

cruiser and several destroyers were dispatched to Japan
after the 1923 Tokyo earthquake, tidal wave.

Son, the shore

was stacked
with bodies,
stacked liked bricks waiting

for the mason. I thought I'd
never eat again after that heavy stench.

They're not the same

as us, he said, and went on, especially when drunk, as to
the misery in the Chinese cities,

so many people living

on boats they boarded-up

as little houses. Death means nothing to them,
nothing. Why in Korea, a buddy told me,

the Chinese

brigades charged into battle in huge waves,
charged with horns and bugles—many weaponless.
He said they were everywhere he looked
with the binoculars.

You can go, go

like a match on a cold night.

Mother said they

used large swabs to smear the ointment
on her head and they attached small metal plates,
lines leading to the electro-shock machine.

Her hands

and ankles were strapped down, a rubber-bit put in her mouth
before they turned on the switch.

Like a blackboard, she's

like a blackboard after they're done, Dad said.
It erases her depression.

Memory like chalk, her
talk—when they allowed her to come home
for a few days from St. Elizabeth's Hospital—
tentative,
                    seeking an image to hold to.
I imagine the two
                    of them in those first nights as they sweated,
called out from their thrusting sex, sipped whiskey
and she listened to him reminisce about the treees
in deepest Virginia.
                    I'll tell you one thing you better remember.
Don't ever let another man
                              knock you
to the floor without getting back up
on your feet and taking it like a man.
You'll get your ass kicked
and you'll kick ass in your time, son.
                              She purchased a can
          of light blue paint
          at a sale. By the time my sister returned home
          from school, she told me, Mom had painted
                                        two tables,
          the radio and my statue
                         of the Blessed Mother Mary. She
said she didn't believe in Hell because she was living
it here on earth.
                    Purgatory, she said, was where her baby boy,
second child, was with all the other little babies
that died so early.
                    They'd gone to New York, weeks before they
married, and Dad took her to a highbrow, fancy restaurant for
dinner. So they ate big time,
                              as Dad would say, and Mom—Bless
          her soul, son; she didn't know better—lifted
          the finger bowl and drank the lemon juice before I
          could say anything.
                              Once, during a two month binge,
          down on money, he put on mother's flowered housecoat,
took a table from the living room and axed it in the backyard—
          cussed and damned everyone . . . like the sailor she said
          he would always be.

I felt so proud with your mother
holding onto my arm. Boy, she was stunning. I drove
to her house with her nephew—he worked as a machinist
at the newspaper with me—and that was the day
we first met. She was so soft, slender, quiet; had a laugh
that affected anyone around. I've never felt
that way about any woman
and I've been with many
a woman in my time.
He always said there
had to be a God. That you could read all the books
you wanted,
travel anywhere in the world, and you'd still
have to look to the sky,
ask yourself how
all those planets and stars got there—accept someone
had to create that beauty; that it just didn't happen
by itself.
There's a juxtaposition, a rhyme
and a reason. Hold a rose, feel and smell
the petals, he said,
and you hold God in your
hand. Pray, pray for your mother to get better
son. Say your prayers and always remember your mother,
me.
He is in the hospital bed and I walk to the edge
of the parking lot. There are tubes about him,
a "full moon above" as he wrote in one
of his country songs. A lone rabbit,
remarkably, feeds
on the grass as over the ridge two streams of red
and white lights move on the beltway.
One Christmas he
brought home a full California Case
as a present and showed me how to hold
the line-gauge firmly, read the characters
for printing by the finger-tip grooves in them.
Now this is a
blank space,
this an Em space. Gutenberg printed the Bible
just this way, he said.

77

I see her at the window,
chain-smoking, and remember, years later,
                              her cardiac death:
            seeing her in the face of the inward, large
            woman, blue bandanna,
in the hospital lobby.
                    I drank then, got drunk that night.
There is the fog on the Potomac River
and two old black men fish
            by the wall. A small fire burns in a halved
            gasoline barrel.
                            Dad said catfish were good eat'n
            if you fried them the right way. Catfish bones,
            black-dotted bones of dice rolling
                                        in the stairwell
            of the steps behind the warehouse on Fifth Street.
Throw them bones. Man, don't hold the dice.
I ain't got all day for your nickel
and dime jive.
            Hey, hey—got to pay the rent,
            put food on that table.
                            She said Grandfather Flynn
got drunk on election day when Al Smith
was defeated so badly—
                    passed out in a snow bank. Two weeks
later he died from pneumonia. He built seven houses
for his children in the neighborhood, each one near
to the other.
            I'll never forgive your father for drinking away
that $5,000 from the house my father left to me. It was gone
in a few months, not a penny left.
                            There is a holy card
            in my first-grade Missal that she put there.
            I sometimes hear her voice in song,
                                        want to kiss
            the hand that brushed away the hair
            from my forehead, damp after a bath.
                            I want you
to get better, to get well. I don't want you to leave
and go back there. I don't like you being there
with all those crazy people, Momma,

and hearing those screams;
them people picking at their skin
like you said some of them do.
Dust of bricks. Tin
awning roof over the coal
shed, latched door. To go into the backyard,
snow along the way to the door—and kick,
kick again. Get rats!
Get! Get out of here!
Lift-up, open and shovel
small pieces at the bottom,
near the spouted pail. They are gone,
hidden. Somewhere light touches
their eyes.
Now Agnes, I'm not going to
play that number. It came up last week. The license tag in
the dream had a seven and a four—that's that. Ok. Seven,
four, eight—just one dollar until payday.
It's cold
and President Kennedy is at the Capitol for his
inauguration. Breaths of the crowds rise away. An old
man, the poet Robert Frost, reads a poem.
By the long avenue
of that day, aloft on the huge muscles
of the sculptured man taming a horse,
from
that statue seeing Kennedy pass by, watching
the old men touch their hearts to fields away.
Little ones waving.
Dad said this life is all
we have. All those people with those big houses, cars, and
money. Sad, son, so many of them forgetting where they came
from.
You look up and there's an apple on a tree, a pear.
So much from a single seed.
Mold, slice of white bread.
Green, blue. Magnifying glass above
the shoots.
Fr. Connor climbed the few stairs
to the pulpit, lecturn. He bowed

to the altar, to us. Rows on rows
of candles. The green of trees
and holly, wreaths tied: bright red bows.
Christmas and choir, old woman's
rosary raised

with cupped hands,
her tongue waiting for new life. The aisles
full.

Sweep the sky of clouds and turn,
glide down by the paths
along the river;

traverse of paddle boats, wake, cherry
blossoms.

Ice! Ice! Nice ice right here! Ice!
Ice! Clean, clean ice here!

The sparked wires
of streetcars on Pennsylvania Avenue a block away—
large black woman loudly preaching
the Bible at the corner: Right in this book. It's
all in these sacred pages for you to read and pray
upon. You're lonely,

you need someone, somebody. He's
the Way. He's the One. All
the sheep went to Him
where He stood.

Cobweb in the small room at the rear
of the house. The small ones with her
on the trembling realm she has spun. She
the sun on their galaxy.

Well, all I know
is he hasn't been back to her and those kids
for more than a week now Mrs. Cox. She's working
two jobs.

The church is empty. The carved door of saints
is open. A pigeon is trapped inside.

I'm a first-
grader. I line up in the line for first-graders.
We're in the school yard. A nun stands at the head
of each line. They speak softly and ritually nod
to each other.

Oh, Sister Anne—please show this little

80

girl to her line. And your name? Anne, too? Oh, but no e. So
your mother told you that? Here, right here
with the others.

> Now I lay me down to sleep.
> I pray the Lord,
> my soul to keep.
> If I should die, before I wake,
> I pray the Lord my soul to take.

The Korean astronomer. He lived on the third floor at the front
with his wife, infant son.

> Some clear nights he set up
> his telescope in the wide space
> between the apartment buildings. I
> stood by, waited, and said nothing. He said
> come here, be careful, don't touch
> the telescope and just stare through
> the lens. It's Mars. It was there.

The night
angel sleeps beside, beside the bed, near
the partially open window. The curtains
are her wings. She protects. The Archangel Michael
watches, too. He has long blond hair and wears
a tight green and yellow-striped
swimsuit beneath his robe. He moves near
as I touch myself under the covers and then turns away.

Penance
> will be the Our Father five times
> and then you must walk the Stations.
Now go, be a good boy, You are forgiven.

Check the stove. Hide
> the bottle of sleeping pills and the razor blades.
> Look in on her, watch for cigarettes. Give her
> one Equanil. Don't stay up too late.

The older boy
has his hand on her leg, her hand inside
his open shirt.

> The sky at last light. Peninsular realms
> of clouds, black flecked path of birds.

                                                        This
          was taken of Aunt Sis with a boyfriend,
          one of many. Look at that hat! That's him,
          his foot on the running board.
                                        Rows of altar boys
on the steps of St. James Church, white cassocked,
their slick hair parted simply.
                              Dan, the one who gassed himself,
                              shut tight all the windows
that summer night.
                    Robert, he was with the submarines.
                                                        She is
the sister of Margaret, the girl with the tapeworm.   You
remember that story. Her sister said the girl
could hold a piece of popcorn to her open mouth
and the tapeworm darted out, would snap it away.
                                              Let us pray
          for those gone. Let us bow our heads in the House
          of Our Lord. Offer your thanks to Him
          who has given us this day.
                                    Grandmother carried
          one of her babies around on a white pillow. It
was so weak and died after three months.
                                        Those mountains
                    in the summer. Then, boy, the fall.
                    Quilt of abundant trees
and from a ridge the lush valley.
Foxes roaming nearby.
                        Past, way of the dream. This waking,
          tremor of pipes in the cold night.
                                    It was her,
                                    she was there.
                                              I miss
          her, boy. Two days ago I was reading the newspaper,
          finished the cup of instant coffee
          and I turned to the kitchen,
          called
                    your mother: Baby, honey,
                    would you mind making me
                    another cup of cof. . .

                              82

Part of

"The entire ocean
is affected by a pebble."

o Blaise Pascal

Part One: Beginning

"If there is a feeling that something has been lost, it may be because much has not yet been used, much is still to be found and begun."

o Muriel Rukeyser

At Dawn

When we wake to the alone before dawn,
from fleet dream and sound of breath,
all we love rises with the orient light.

Through the silence by the near window,
on the arch of sparrows between trees,
we live and feel again—hope from doubt.

The Great Star of our pulses, the seas,
hidden messenger revealed after dark,
caresses our planet, touches all we see.

By the life of the gnat and the blossom,
voice of another, some remembered face,
we will go our way, at dawn enter the day.

Seeing

I recall removing the cork top
from the narrow vial of shrimp eggs
when ten and then gently tapping a few
to the water on the smooth-edged slide.

I slipped the slide under thin metal grips
that could break if bent back too far
and repeated softly: I can do this—
close my left eye and not use a hand.

I stared into the microscope and a blur
mirrored in my receptive right eye.
I adjusted the grooved black knobs
and two circles eclipsed to form one
where the curved eggs were.

I wanted some thing to live, push out,
escape from within and swim free.

After the Rent

On payday, after the rent
and checking of other cares,
Dad sometimes would bring Mom
a box of Schrafft's assorted candy
or flowers coned in his right hand—
the wrapping paper thin, vulnerable as the orphan
in the sheer brown of his eyes.

Home after several drinks,
he would stand before her,
like a small boy watching
the Richmond sky clear for the first time, and say:
"Mama, these are for you."

To My Lost Brother

James Edward Cox
3/25/41-10/24/41

You lived, struggled for seven months, Mom said,
and, born clubfooted, you died from pneumonia
after the surgeons separated your twisted feet
from the subtle spine. She visited almost daily
by bus and streetcar through those three seasons.

In the bitter winter before your birth, she slipped,
fell hard from the ice-covered curb. Her grief
was your brief time here—loss of her second child,
first son—and a future, had you lived, confined
to a wheelchair, dependent on others, incontinent.

The nurses and doctors took special care, she said,
looked in on you during their rounds, routine tasks,
and, warmed by your smile from the domed white crib,
told how you turned to the least gesture, gentle tap.

Jim, Ed, James, Edward, Eddie, Jimmy, Jimmy Boy,
Eddie Boy, Brother, she missed you terribly,
as they say, and her hands revealed your loss:
fidgets, nails chewed, and fingers arched away.

They buried you in the city-owned potters field,
Mom said, in a remote plot, near the Anacostia River,
because they had so little then, no money to spare.
She believed you were not forever bound to Limbo
but, since you died beyond the womb, away in Heaven.

The Faith

My Aunt Mary, Mamie, a good and true Flynn,
steeped in her deep love of the Blessed Virgin,
brewed tea three times from the same bag;
laced them to the kitchen windowlock to dry
as the deaths of World War II raged over Europe,
the vast Pacific, daily headlined newspapers.
In the parlor photographs of two uniformed sons,
a choir of nephews, graced the table beneath
the always watchful eyes of the Sacred Heart.

She worked for years in the narrow aisles
of the gift store at the Old Shrine; dusted
the exquisitely clad Infant of Prague,
tidied holy cards, and uttered prayers
for the family, those so dear, far away.

Together

My mother taught me to embrace
simple tasks: to crease and fold
each sheet in a particular way.

"We'll do this together, Eddie-Boy,"
and we gathered the loads of clothes—
careful to avoid the hot zippers,

surge of sparks across sweaters—
from the rows of laundromat dryers.
I sailed with her in the billowed white

and blue order. She sang the voice
of the day's troubles, brushed the hair
from my eyes when I pressed to her side.

Family

I put the phone down after a long talk
with my sister Laura about our jobs,
her two sons, recalling the Thanksgiving
Dad got drunk, grabbed the uncarved turkey
and bit into the crisp brown side.
We sat with Mom at the fully set table,
and, unable to cry anymore, we laughed—laughed.

In 1966 you were in the busy White Tower
diner on 11th Street with classmates, girls
from St.Patrick's Academy. They joked,
sipped cold coffee, puffed smudged cigarettes,
and brushed shiny, imitation leather jackets.

It's past midnight and the wind sounds
against the house. My room is the ship—
overhauled minesweeper—I never set
from shore on when stationed in Japan
and Laura, for three hours after school,
filed glossies of senior graduating class
while I stood inspection near the rice fields.

Names

We looped and carefully guided the string
through two triangular holes in the dented,

empty beer can and tied several knots.
The can was balanced on the front fender

of a parked car and the line, sagging across
the narrow asphalt street, was drawn tight;

the far end bound to the parked car opposite.
We crouched, held in our glee, and waited

for someone to drive by and be snared,
like the Piper airplane in the serial movie.

Near the intersection we heard gears shift
and then a car sped into the hidden prank.

You were supposed to feign alarm, run beside
the driver's window, and shout: "Hey, Mister,

your hubcap fell off! Your hubcap fell off!"
I yelled carburetor and learned, by shove

and bony elbow, to shout the right word:
how things have names, a meaning of their own.

Passing It On

When the thunderstorm roared, tried her nerves,
Grandmother Flynn burned blessed votive candles,
prayed the rosary and sang the songs of longing
for family, her red-haired cousins in Ireland.
Grandfather, a dairyman and staunch Democrat,
made passage several times and, upon return,
placed peat moss, green ribbon bow-tied,
in her hands. She kissed, cherished the gifts.

My mother Agnes, frail, youngest of sixteen,
stayed at Grandmother's side, talkative ways,
repeated, kept the stories and sayings alive.

In the cafeteria, downtown, she whispered
as I watched a man twitch, laugh to himself:

> "You shouldn't stare at people
> who are crippled and epileptic.
> God will punish you if you do,
> for sure, and make you the same."

The Saturday afternoon movie matinee my desire,
"Just a quarter" my plea, she'd playfully say:

> "Don't spend it all in one place
> and don't take any wooden nickels.
>
> Wish in one hand, shit in the other,
> and see which one fills up first."

She spoke a litany, leaving for Eastern Market,
and said, after I'd asked if I, too, could go:

> "I wouldn't take you
> to a dogfight
> dressed like that.
>
> People in hell
> want ice water.

I'm going crazy.
You want to come along?"

In bed, lights turned off, after she counted
the wee little piggies of my toes, I'd pray
the way she taught me to do—hands steepled:

"Now I lay me down to sleep,
I pray the Lord my soul to keep.
If I should die before I wake,
I pray the Lord my soul to take."

She'd hug me, kiss my forehead, and say:

"Sleep tight and don't let
the bedbugs bite."

"These African violets," she once lamented,
"are so hard to grow—no matter what I do."
They seldom blossomed twice but she tried,
hoped to discover the bright yellow center,
years later, I'd learn to call the anther.

Part Two: Each Other

"Two who are Mostly Good.
 Two who have lived their day,
 But keep on putting on their clothes
 And putting things away."

o Gwendolyn Brooks

One

They wait at the crowded corner curb
for the yellow light to turn green.
He balances, grips the aluminum walker
as she stands proudly with wood cane.
How long have these two been together?
Who numbers colds and dreams revealed?

She found him sprawled on the floor
after the second of the serious falls.
He moaned, held the injured leg, and
rested his head against the tub.

No matter where they go he opens the door.
Life continues for them like a dance:
first this step, then the next: one, two;
one, two; one, I'm here with, for you.

Waiting

I've no idea or sense of place
what it is you see as you stare
across the crowded bar. Your eyes
have found some space I can't see:
rooms you've slept in, long streets,
the face of one you met here before.

You bend your head and look up
whenever the door sounds to open
and close over the song played
three times. Few minutes pass
before you pull twice at the cuff
of the red plaid shirt, check
the watch on your tattooed wrist.

I wait and stall for this man
I believe—tell myself and write
in letters to distant friends—
will enter and then sit, turn
to find the words of my hands.

Search

I lift the window-shade to the rays
of afternoon sun and the empty cup,
saucer, spoon, and curved shadows.

On the tin garage roof in the alley,
after two days of snow, the birds
feed on crackers and wheat bread.

The squirrel burrows at the roof's edge,
hunts for food long buried. She lifts
her head in the alchemy of air and water
and light plays back, falls, drifts up.

Bulbs Live On

In the snowstorm the young homeless man
　　　　stretches over the vent; steam
　　　　surrounds his sleeping space.

Somewhere tense soldiers unload the truck,
　　　　guards stand at ready. The weapon,
　　　　mysterious, can destroy an entire city.

It's possible to see yourself in the mirror,
　　　　remember your face as a child; hear
　　　　the window shut, the voice of a fear.

The woman waits and the man waits. They wait
　　　　for the other to say anything. She imagines
　　　　the day they first met, the two yellow roses.

The old woman, ninety-three, walks to the door,
　　　　buttons her coat. Even in coldest winter,
　　　　she says, the bulbs live on in the earth.

Departure

Toward the close of day
the old man wakes.
He lingers in bed,
watches the window and listens
to the traffic on the street.
He rises, unfolds brown pants
from the back of the chair.

There are the stairs.
They step into the kitchen,
lead to the screened porch.
He stands in frames of light.

When it rains
he sometimes crouches
and bends low,
presses his face
to the smooth grain floor.
He's the neighbor's children,
birds flying into tall buildings,
the time his wife—
for nearly an hour—
stood outside their first house.

When he pushed down
the gas pedal she turned,
walked to the fully packed van
they'd rented, and said
she didn't see how people
could do it time and again:
the leaving, being alone.

Entwined

A map courses in the minute realm, life beyond
translucent geographies of multiplying cells;
green bread mold, this limbless phallus terrain
swayed by a molecular wind. In calmest dark,
beside, in sleep, I moved my exposed body beneath
the upper window, a seclusion of several stars.

Waved traffic echo, pipe surge, radiator hiss,
intimate tract of rooms, fleshed imprints, hands
wall-papered, painted over. There, two standing,
they mouth at the rear of the near quiet house:
pulse, sweat entwined, last touch, pillow, tuck.

Cuddle the Bricks

He be you, he say. He be me, he say.
He said even the moon, in time, reaches
the sewer and waves of light sail the water,
enter side tunnels. That is what he said.
He did. He did. He said voices speak
in the bunched leaves and that salvation
is wrapped in his belongings, skin bruised
from weathered ropes, muscles torn.

He raised his head and said: I am you,
as you are me in the misery of these avenues
and streets. Cuddle the bricks, whisper
beneath the great map of stars.

Passenger

The escalator descends and I try to call out
the names, places as they surface within me.
Sometimes, in the rush hour crowds, I shout
so all who listen can hear my deepest plea.
A sound tunes at my ears and I rise to my feet,
walk with others in the just illuminated night.
The leaves of full trees carpet the wet street
and I head homeward on steps of dark and light.
Hours circle the day toward its nearing end,
and the city, light by light, enters into sleep.
Tomorrow is yet another time when I might mend
the losses I travel with, must always keep.
>   This I say, to you and you, is all I know.
>   I am a passenger, hear me—listen as I go.

Part Three: Common Good

"We have all known the long loneliness
 and we have learned the only solution
 is love and that love comes from community."

o Dorothy Day

Her Recounting

for Robert Coles

I felt his hair against my face
when I prayed, knelt before rows
of candles, guttering red lights.

His long fingers gently covered
the blotches of my spotted hand,
pulsed life as a small animal does.

He spoke of a place, glorious room,
in the far house which is his home.
Listen, he consoled, the door opens,

blind men speak colors, the mute talk,
and the lame walk from their shadows,
the braces and canes falling away.

Benediction

Let us receive and embrace those who must find
temporary shelter under the canopy of a tree:
a place, room of shrubs, and the abandoned car.

May the grass be lush and dry, gently comfort
the homeless in their sleep; insects alien
to an exposed face—folded, bare-veined arms.

Stay the rain and gathering islands of clouds,
protect the weary wherever they seek rest.
Be with them, we pray, in the near, approaching far.

Throughout the Day

1. Bus Stop

The young woman
stands in the cold,
says to her small son:
"Hold your head up
so the wind won't blow
on your neck."

2. Duet

In the bright sun
of mid-afternoon
two sparrows,
from opposite ledges,
sing and sway
as those nearby
turn to their sound.

3. Dead Moth

Your wings tremble
on the curtain
when they dynamite
for the subway.

The Wanderer

It begins after sleep and I wake
on the damp ground. The cut grass
covers my clothes and small rocks
stick to my face, arms, elbows.
I get up, pack my things, and walk
to wherever it is that I must go.

I'm always trying to speak and say
something I never seem to understand.
I hold the phone in the crowded drugstore
and talk out loud so they will think
I'm talking to someone on the other end.

There's money in the green glass bottles
people drink from in the park at noon,
that I gather at construction sites.

In the evening, on my chosen park bench,
I hear music, many singing far away—
like Sunday mornings, when just a boy,
as I walked with my mother to pray.

These Clouds

Monet, you stilled two clouds on the canvas
for us and eighty-four years later I open
a book of lithographs to another continent,
reflections at the center of the pond:
lilies, several red-hued blossoms adrift.

They are white inverted realms: one large
and the other, at left, a smaller entity
in the sky you placed your belongings under—
slowly let go the bag of brushes, pallet,
and rolled tubes. You left us another view.

From the high wind you captured this light
and turned the world around for the many
who rise in computerized elevators, stare
at televised hearings and the canting man,
anxious, who sweats to the whir of cameras.

I see you step back, forward, to slowly guide
the brush to the bushes and thickened shore.
The grass, a green mist, flourishes stalks
as you intended them to grow. The waters
swirl the vortex, your eyes: everything flows.

Testimonies

My mother sits at the kitchen table,
steadily puffs on a menthol cigarette,
and talks of the tragic train crash
at Union Station several years before:

"People screamed and they ran
 when the speeding train crashed
 through the wall, fell
 loudly to the floor on the next level.
 Many were killed and many
 of the badly injured later died."

   ✻   ✻   ✻   ✻

Mrs. Little spoke of her dearest friend
from the river town where they were born:

"She gave birth to twins and Ana,
 a midwife, said it strained her so.
 She took cold and always talked
 of the past. A younger sister,
 from another town, raised the babies.
 We found her alone one day, counting
 nails in the side of the empty barn.
 She begged for her children.

They sent her to a hospital in Georgia.
 We'd rent a car and drive down to visit
 for a day or so. From the iron-gate
 entrance we'd follow the paved road
 to a bunch of houses, large buildings
 surrounded by a high fence and trees.

The nurse said she was in the field
 picking strawberries and, for weeks,
 she'd been saying, though fifty-five,
 that she would soon be eighty-two."

   ✻   ✻   ✻   ✻

A short woman, middle-aged, neatly dressed,
stood at the curb on Pennsylvania Avenue
and yelled to all who passed her spot:

"I mean, I thought, I believed,
 a woman was supposed to have
 the same damn right to work–
 just the same as any man!"

   ✻   ✻   ✻   ✻

Jeffrey, four, the muscle of his heart
tightening toward an early death, said:

"I was a little, small dolphin
 and then I got out of the water
 and walked into the big house."

   ✻   ✻   ✻   ✻

In the summer she sat on the brick wall
by the market and mumbled aloud.
Her large legs, festered with open sores,
partially wrapped in darkened bandages,
were swollen and caked with blood.

Years later, near the half-way house
for mental patients, she stood, faced
the morning sun and tossed
balled bread to the sparrows.

   ✻   ✻   ✻   ✻

All the great animals kneel down to die.
Their breaths drift through the night,
settle on the plains. Their eyes
reveal memories of full water holes.

The Test

In this essay section of the test
you're required to write scenarios
from your earliest memory.

You will not be judged by the written,
only by the unspoken of your face.
There is no necessity to document

names, a particular place or time.
What matters is that you portray,
as accurately as you can, feelings

and the status of the hunger felt
in your soul, the sheer realities
of hurt, anger—even minor defeat.

There's no time requirement or grade
in the completion of this examination.
The entire test can be taken with you

to the place where you currently live.
You're allowed to weep over the pages,
use them to wipe sweat from your brow.

It's impossible to fail this test.
You are only required to do your best.
Your life, somehow, will be revealed

by the lead of the pencil, black pen,
between the light blue lined pages.
Start, resume writing when you wake.

The Trapped Whales

The solitary leaf falls
as I walk after midnight.
Thousands of dark miles away,

yet near as the faint hum
of electric breath turning
in the alarm clock, I hear,

see the three of you rise,
on the 60-second segment
of the Sunday evening news,

from the narrowest opening
in the thick ice
somewhere in northern Alaska.

The arctic cold now hinders,
the announcer says,
the man, mustache whitened,

who uses a chain-saw to cut
away slabs of ice—not fleeing
teenagers in a horror film—

in this effort to stall time.
You must surface frequently,
he adds, to suck in the air

and, in sequence, like pumps
beside the transplanted heart,
you three are a singular rhythm

in this great struggle against
the odds, and day's fading light.
The man, stretched on his stomach,

clings to the edge, reaches
to stroke your wounded heads
when you swim close. In the spray

of your exhaled breath, his own,
he longs—as chance viewers pray—
for you, himself, all near death.

117

Mary in November

You see, dear sir, I'm a street evangelist.
I've tried to live by and preach the Bible.
When a patient at St. Elizabeth's Hospital,
place where they held that poet Ezra Pound,
the young doctor said I was sick from Jesus.

Sir, there will be so many homeless people
in the city when winter, the snow arrives.
I know lots of these souls. I gave a pair
of brown pants to this one man who sleeps
on the vents down by the State Department.
If I have the change, I'll give them some
for that cup of coffee—strong and black.

People seldom appreciate a gift, though.
I gave fifty cents to a woman at the corner
and she spent it all by the end of the day.
I try to stretch what I have, make it last.

I stood in the comfort of the heated entrance
to the new condominium, to escape the cold,
and this uniformed security guard told me
I had to leave, said I had to move on.

You wonder why people act in such a way.
I read a magazine article on why clothes,
especially furs, are so in fashion today.
There's waste practically everywhere I go.
Yet I can find a full meal of vegetables
in the restaurant dumpster after dark.

There's more work to be done, many tasks
important to do. In the shelter kitchen,
where they give you soup and a sandwich,
I'll get warm some, then be on my way;
the Lord Jesus beside me on these streets.

On the Lake

In the hours before dawn crews repair
the engine rows of fighter planes.
One man holds a lamp, trail of black cord,
as the mechanic wipes away grease, stares,
head cocked, at the finely calibrated part
he labored to loosen, fix and replace.

The planes, readied, line the runway side,
await pilots asleep in aerobatic dreams
of flown missions—blue skies and spans
of clouds liberated from enemy strikes.

Codes pulsate the command center bunker—
magnetic red circles, penny-size, patrol
the geometric grid coast to the occupied,
wild-flowered beaches of Normandy's shore—
and primary, secondary targets are marked.

By longitude and latitude the young airman feels,
again, the passionate night on the lake years past.
The weary pilots tip wings toward the unaccounted,
downed and, forty years later, there are the eyes
of the handsome man in the torn, autumnal newsclip.

Part Four: This Realm

"Time is a storm in which we are all lost.
Only inside the convolutions of the storm
itself shall we find our directions . . .

o William Carlos Williams

Harvard Graduate Speaking
to His Troops

It is important to be approximate.
Maintain a steady hand.
Your eyes should hold the enemy—
    like a small vessel at offertory.
But don't prolong the process.
Too much contemplation,
    a philosophy teacher once confided to me,
    distorts the image.
That is, you begin to think, to dwell:
    dreams and music can stir across
    another man's face if you stall.
Immediacy, then, is the crucial word:
    our primary objective.

Be true to your weapon.
One has to be true to something.

First Hunt

I watch the village
through a forest of rice
and wire barbed with teeth
the mud brown of mountain
and junction stream.

A woman, mouth open, flails
words and arms in the wake
of roar and wings.

I recall the wet breath
of the dying deer I shot
in my seventeenth year
in the fall, in West Virginia.

In the Before

In the before, at some corner passing,
from mute lips of elevatored floors,
near spray of sweat, against the wall,
standing, assured at the cleansed mirror,
I see you in the waveless blue lake of sky.

Three in the Morning

The air then is still, thick.
Dark covers the door and corners,
the walls a blind gallery:
paintings void of frame and face.

You are awake
while others sleep.

This is the time,
moment only you share,
when you touch your chest,
unbutton the shirt.

Light rises between
your fingers.

At the Fountain

In the vivid light of the early morning
the small girl, maybe three, runs before
to the edge of the fountain. Abreast
in brilliant green plumage, three ducks
swim along slowly above the rush-hour din.
She calls out "Look, Mommy—they go, go!"

"Go ducks," she pleads twice, and one glides
the ripple of her voice; his smooth bill
a synapse, silent reply as he turns her way.

The Other Side

From sleep, the much-desired nap,
undershirt wet, I return, slowly move.
The sheet and blanket form a long body
from the dream I traveled through—
close to the people, words they spoke.
I heard a muddled voice across the wide,
turbulent river, and asked, repeatedly,
for what was said from the beginning
to the man beside who wanted to hear.

My grandmother dreamed she witnessed
her mother ascend the clouded Cork sky.
She ran, sought to touch the dress hem
and saw herself in the white lace gown.
Her large arms were smooth, almost clear
of blue needle marks, patches of bruises.
Bedridden, she spoke of heaven's journey,
day and night visions. "I was twelve,"
my mother said, "the day my older sister
found her turned toward the open window."

As she stood on deck, hands at the rail,
my grandmother watched her father shake
his fist from the pier and loudly damn her
for leaving Ireland to work as a maid
for the British, earn passage to America.
Obedient, she vowed, as he bellowed anger,
to obey his command to never again return.

The ship steamed from port, the wake wide
in the morning fog. Grandmother covered
her face, stared to the obscured shore:
O Ireland, Ireland.

I Want to Tell Them

There is a clot at the back of my head,
I know it. I've told them,

more than once, that it is there,
has been present for as long

as I can recall. I noted it the first night.
I told them last night. They just nod

their heads. No one talks directly to me.
All they do is listen, send for a doctor.

She listens, though more attentive,
and leaves. I can feel it each day

when the sky frames the window red;
the setting sun as sure as the words,

all I've said. I taste its hues
in my mouth. My tongue is cloud and wind

with the waste of tissue. I know it.
They know it. There is a clot at the back

of my head—stars, rooms that do not appear
on the charts at the far end of my bed.

Shells of Milk Cartons

The trains are in long lines of cars
and shoots of steam rise beneath
their sleek sides, silver stomachs.
I might travel the highways by bus
during the day and view small towns.
I would arrive by car to the newness
of radio dials and search for music,
clear skies in the weather report.

Where is the answer in the book?
How often do you need to read text,
turn the many white pages again?
Can a sum be given for one loved,
his age, the story she must tell?

The pigeons coo before they glide
from vacant buildings where people
should live, embrace, enter sleep.

The old woman rummages the trash can,
grasps the edge of rusted mesh wire—
stirs paper, shells of milk cartons,
holds the discarded clock to her ear.

The Secret Lives of Animals

From the nowhere of the late, hot afternoon
the sparrow descends, swoops directly down,
and the green-hooded Japanese beetle is askew,

knocked over, the stomach revealed
in the instant force of the arched wings
above the concrete. She grasps the prey tight

in her beak, assumes the air, way beneath
and to the small porch niche where she lives
with her young, their continual calls for food.

In the nest of twigs, leaves, pieces of paper,
they huddle together: offspring to mother,
each beside the other under the clear sky.

The ants shape their tunnels, move tirelessly
where we seldom see them unless a rock is raised
in the woods and the village, hub of translucent

and minute eggs, patterns the earth untouched
by sun. So it is with the bats, those nights
they cast the blind net for mosquitoes, descend

beyond the traffic and apartment buildings
in mass funnel toward the library chimney.
Upside down, one to the next, they sleep.

The young couple kiss behind the garage door,
will sleep hind to leg, arm over breast, chest.

Carnegie Library, Park Bathroom

The wino stands before the mirror, arches his head,
slowly pulls the razor up his soap-lathered neck.
Pieces of towel cover spots where he nicked himself.

The basin is nearly half-filled with water,
splotches of blood, and curled dregs of beard.
His catchy humming in the downstairs bathroom

quiets my awkward entrance. I hear him tap
his right foot, watch as he washes his image
in the smeared glass. In this place, respite

for those of no fixed address, the odor of urine
and cheap drink layers the dank air. He dampens,
then slowly combs back his long and graying hair.

Broken is the Cup

Broken is the cup—blue
and white shard, curved—
surface of calm water,
path of trees, painted inlet
where boats might dock.
The cup held coffee,

tea, fruit of fullest grape;
half-filled, once,
with bourbon when they danced

that day the war finally ended.
This is the fossil of thirst,
vessel into which one stared

through grief, grasped tight
after the dream, called out:
sitting straight-up in bed.

Part Five: Part of

"One feels oneself part of another person
and that other person becomes a part of us."

o Ernesto Cardenal

The Moons of Mars

1.

Along the beach there is the evidence
of galaxies in the sand and rocks,
complexities of minute crabs,
and flash of fish that swam before.
We, too, moved from the water to land
and our memories complete the shore.

2.

The astronomer Asaph Hall peered patiently
into the evolving far, August 17, 1877,
as the telescope roamed the ocean of stars.
Slowly, by adjustment and precise computation,
the planet Mars is centered on the lens surface,
a light to his eyes. This night, though,
there is a shift in the measured range of sight.
His reward is the discovery of the two moons.
Hall charts the positions and names them
from roots in mythology: Phobos and Deimos.

3.

In the night stroll the moon is reflected
on the ocean and stills the walker's steps:
waves annex the shore, are wind echoed.

Last Night

I am the paper-locked equations
mapped on the huge blackboards:
dust of chalk white matter.
Men sit, ponder my many signs,
and drift in the phenomena
of lines, coded calculations.
They absorb my intricate design
and become traitors to life.
The tufts of black hair conceal
the youthful mathematician's brain.
In his cranium my power is fed.

The anxious physicist dreams
she is the one who will travel
in the arched bomber stomach.
Near the plotted destination
he scans the magnified city
captured in the marked lines:
people prune neat garden rows,
a child tugs at his book bag,
and two women sweep stone paths.

I will evolve in seconds,
become the last light seen:
explode, a domed flame.

Behold, I will sear your eyes,
darken any who might witness me.
You shall hear my thunder force
in the firestorm, destroyer wind.
Many will evaporate, only shadows
will reveal where they once stood.

In detonation I am verified
beyond all the original estimates:
Hiroshima, 8:15 a.m., August 6, 1945—
66,000 killed and 100,000 maimed,
wandering in pain, fleeing the fires.

Note for the Fireplace

In this cabin by the bend
in the river we leave the skull
we believe to be that of a fox;
bleached and at final rest
on the fireplace mantel—
no longer pursued by the hunter
as is the hunter by the seasons.

The Composer

In the ever present silence I see a melody
animate, descend and rise along the piano keys.
I listen for a sound, any rhythm I might hear.

Hidden music abides everywhere, waits to be heard.
I pen notes—scale of snow and music of the tree.
In the ever present silence I see a melody.

This faint sound is always near, wherever I go.
I try to compose the elusive tone, measured way.
I listen for a sound, any rhythm I might hear.

I find release in the sleep of the still night,
seek to create harmony by light's return, day.
In the ever present silence I see a melody.

In the rows of faces in the boys' choir, I sang—
mimed the hymn like a fish surfacing for air.
I listen for a sound, any rhythm I might hear.

Beyond traffic, voices on the elevator, phone,
I long to compose, alone, the life I find there.
In the ever present silence I see a melody.
I listen for a sound, any rhythm I might hear.

Your Realm

I await the appearance of your eyes
and will be motionless at your side,
muffle my breathing. I will assume
the stance of passivity due the great
jungle beast, animals of the mountain,
the desert, and not stare directly.

You will surface in the dream quarry,
stand at the open window and long
for your thin wrists to be kissed,
to feel the wet mouth on the nap
of your neck and gasp, let go—
released, finally, in a caress
beyond convoluted news of the day
as the small blip of light vanishes
from the television and last image.

The Vulnerable

Consider the fragile one: human, animal,
plant, and insect—the precarious thing
which, by mere circumstance, continues
because we choose to place it there.

At birth the kangaroo's issue, blood wet,
cover of sack—twig of the leaping tree—
must crawl the terrain of thick fur
to the pouch, feed from the nipple
for six months, be nurtured and grow.
It does not see and yet moves on smell,
magnificence of this instinct to survive.

The woman has paced the wards for years
and the doctors, nurses, maintenance man,
know her by name. In the small cloth bags
she carries a missal, brush, powder tin,
lipstick, cigarettes. Fading puffs trail
her steps. Moment by moment, hour by day,
month by year, she has obeyed the rules
and stood by the window. She is cautious
in waxed hallways, a stroll of mowed lawns,
and kneels in the chapel for daily prayers;
waits on her husband to arrive, take her away.
She anguishes for the old man they strapped
in the wheelchair, the trapped bee, a fly.

The Edge

For those at the edge the light switch
is flicked off but the blub glares on
in the darkened room of elusive sleep.

They measure by minute and hour, needs,
small tasks, in getting through the day.
Their longing is money to meet the rent,

food and milk to last the week. By joke,
tight embrace, and most passionate kiss,
they make do with syrup for coffee's sugar.

Voices

Little Boy:

O, you little bug thing you. You little.
You green and kind of yellow, too. Where
you fly? Where you go? Where you live?
Take me with you, little bug.

Older Boy in Field:

The ball might be hit in the air soon.
Look up but hold your hand to the sun.
The pitcher bends from the mound, the pitch
a white trail to the batter, and all you
can do is wait for the sacrifice play.

The Old Woman:

We walked down to the swollen river. Trees
and branches covered the shore. There had been
a sudden storm and much rain. We searched
for my husband by torch for hours.

One of the Mourners:

The priest signed a cross in the air,
said Amen, and a silence persisted
in the hands of damp earth tossed
toward the coffin, room of the ground.
The gathered breathed memory.

The Mother:

I was the vessel in the dream and rowed steadily,
my baby at the bow of the boat. The placenta net
was our bed. By the voice, grace I speak to
in the isolated dark, I increased, released
the one who waves my name.

Moving

It is quiet in the large room.
I sit on a box of packed books

and stare at the bare walls
where shadows of tape remain:

patterns from the poster
of the Spiral Galaxy in Antlia.

Around the white woodwork edges
is the dust, hidden so long

by bookshelves and the table
where the coleus plants grew.

I dwell on how life unfolded
in this room, my four-year home.

Behind the surface of the eyes,
by the root paths of the brain,

I recall, remember, am reminded
of one seated in the brown chair.

Later, I will stand, carry the box,
look back, finally lock the door.

The Work Sweater

A skilled linotypist, my father would save
randomly set errors: erotic, transposed letters,
absurd late season batting averages. He stowed
the burred lines in the weighted-down pockets
of his red, green and blue cardigan sweater—
the fifty-year union pin worn to the left.

Biblically, Baptist bred, his given name Ezra,
he would sway, preach after several drinks.
He sermoned parables of juxtaposed stars—
God's presence in the backyard trees.

Words, their usage, sounds, embellished the poems
he secretly typeset, we found after his death,
hidden in a folder in the neatly ordered dresser:

Old Man

Old man, with pace so slow
Past my home each day you go
And deep within I feel it
    strong . . .
For me also it won't be long
Till someone, too, will watch
    me go
Past their home with pace so
    slow.
The trees now shorn of spring
    attire
Deep down their roots fused
    with desire
To be born again as in the
    past . . .
Old man, shorn trees, the die
    is cast
And time will pass as it always
    must
And those who walk now will
    be nought but dust.

o Ezra Cox

He mused at the oddities borne of his stray touch:
errant curve balls surely fielded by callused hands.
His Joseph's garment, repository for lead line mistakes,
gradually gave to the stitched past, unraveling threads.
Sober or drunk, he was a respected, good friend.
He firmly grasped the shoulder of one of the men
on the picket line of a winter strike and clearly
spoke his chosen words of condolence to the man
who grieved his dead wife. Instinct circled
his horse tips, notes for fast and slow tracks
on the densely set pages of *The Daily Racing Form*.
His hands signed the news of union negotiations
in the gasoline fumed air, his face mirroring
the receptiveness of a deaf woman at an open locker.

I wear his work sweater, the two pockets sewn
sure again, and see his graced, supple fingers
hover the square plateaus of linotype keys,
lever high lines of finely teethed, copper mats.
Over the press deadline surge he could hear
someone approach and turned to smile and say:
"Where you been all my life, buddy? A dollar
on that number again? Make it to the track?
Sam, it's not the same trade it was back then."

Alone again, he'd sip a third cup of coffee,
light another cigarette, set it down and adjust
his sweater. The chair and cushion steady,
he positioned deft piston fingers as a pianist does,
head bowed slightly to the waiting conductor.

Part of

I.   The Gift

Near the down escalator pouring the rush hour crowd to the subway,
the old homeless man stands, layered by frayed emblems of cloth.
Red stocking-capped, he stares intently but does not ask, reach.
Medieval mendicant, silent, he waits for one to slow and stop,
hear the growls, and turn to heed the obvious hunger in his eyes.

Direct from the hurried exchange the young broker, cosmopolitan,
numbed by sales, tabular quotations of the green computer screen,
retrieves the pocket's day change for the waiting, soil-faced man.
He empties coins into cupped, weathered hands and then nods,
walks away, recalls the coal mines—his father's mask of soot.

> Within are the hidden words I will need to hear
> and speak when night's cycle concludes the day.
> I seek the way of hope, by love to face my fear:
> be part of when I can give, receive, draw near.

II.   The Receiver

My father, eighteen, departed ten years of frequent boyhood fights
at a Baptist orphanage deep in Virginia. Apprenticed a printer,
he went on to join the Navy. Handsome, white-uniformed, he danced,
smoked opium in Shanghai, saw Tokyo after the 1923 earthquake.
"The ocean waves," he said, "lulled the night watch to sleep."

Once, as I readied for school, he returned to the apartment
from the nearby bus stop, his forehead riveted by thought,
and rubbed his face, stared at barren trees in the alley.
Mamma, damp towel at her waist, asked: "What happened Daddy?"
"This old man collapsed—a heart attack—died right in my arms."

> Speak when night's cycle concludes the day.
> Seek your way of hope and by love thwart fear.
> Be a part of as you receive, give, draw near
> to the hidden in the words you need to hear.

148

III.   The Forgotten

At noon, in the grocery store, when no one turns, looks her way,
the destitute mother siphons a milk for her feeble child.
The woman from El Salvador prays over brittle grains of rice
on the manna floor. A black youth, arm taut, mainlines ammonia;
another rubs his AIDS stigmata, longs to cipher the acronym.

Stuporous with blue Valium, a woman stands by the sink and weeps—
wet hands tremble in dawn light. The radiant pregnant girl,
sixteen, bears seed, a fatherless child—her heart beats for two.
Racked by strokes, eighty-one, the man pours hoarded sleeping pills.
Ten years less, near blind, his wife holds their covenant of water.

> They seek a way of hope and by love thwart fear,
> are a part of when they give, receive, draw near.
> Within are the hidden words they yearn to hear,
> speak when night's cycle concludes their day.

IV.   The Remembered

Who has not lost one loved, seen silence in the tinted photograph?
Beckoned by dreams, we pursued them on repeating, wasted streets.
Hostages to neither heaven nor hell, they continue on in our world.
They are the strangers we see when we sip coffee at the corner café,
observe a passerby, recall a friend near death, his final days.
In this life, Moon companion to the Earth—orb of influence, tide—
we are responsible to those who seek our care and need our love.
Archivists, we image dust's blest matter of the many who have died.
Our duty, sure as breath, is to embrace the fellow survivors here,
all we are part of and, by the gift of life, revere the dead.

> To become part of them we give, receive, draw near.
> Within are hidden words they spoke, we need to hear,
> and speak when the night cycle of our life ends the day.
> We seek their way of hope and by love we conquer fear.

Photo by Robert W. Witt

Ed Cox: A Biographical Note

Where does a poem come from? Half the answer is that it comes from one who stops, looks, and listens. Ed Cox spent most of his life stopping, looking, and listening, almost from the day he was born in Washington, D.C., in 1946 and taken home to a house on Capitol Hill where his earliest memories were shaped. He had more than thirty addresses after that first childhood home, but all of them–except for four years he spent in the Navy, stationed first in Tokyo and then in Baltimore–were in and around Washington.

Monumental Washington, though, played little part in Ed's poetic imagination. The politics that enspirited him and shaped his work is the politics of human encounter, the politics that rises from the outrage fired by one person's cruelty and carelessness toward another, and from the joy that suffuses the sharing of a common meal or the gift of a glass of cool water, and from the conviction that anyone and everyone can do something to enrich our life together.

Ed acquired his poet's tools first at Archbishop John Carroll High School, from which he was graduated in 1964, then in a semester's study with poets Rudd Fleming and Roderick Jellema at the University of Maryland, and finally under a rigorous program of self-directed education that led him through poetry classical and contemporary, philosophy, theology, and criticism, and continued

150

unabated to the end of his life. Two early books of poetry, *Blocks* and *Waking*, were published in 1972 and 1977. "These Two: Ezra and Agnes," a prose poem about his parents, appeared in October-November 1989 in *The Washington Review*. Those works reappear in this volume along with the full text of *Part of*, a sequence of poems whose writing and rewriting occupied the last dozen years of his life. The poems of *Part of*, like Ed's earlier work, are distilled from the events of a life of activism as reflected upon in times of intervening solitude. Starting with the antiwar organizing that he began while still in the Navy, Ed combined writing with advocating and working for social change. In the late 1960s and early 1970s he was active in promoting public nonacademic poetry, working with a collaborative of poets who called themselves the Some Of Us Press. Beginning in 1976 he organized and led a number of poetry workshops for old people; he collected and edited two anthologies of his students' work, *Seeds and Leaves* (1977) and *Some Lives* (1984).

Like most poets Ed had to engage in "bread-labor" over the years to support his poetic endeavors. For the most part this was as an administrator in cultural and public interest organizations, among them the National Council on the Arts, Common Cause, the Indochina Refugee Action Center, the National Center for Urban Ethnic Affairs, and the United States Association for the United Nations High Commissioner for Refugees. In addition to his books, his poems appeared in the *Sewanee Review, December, Calvert Review, The Washington Post* and other publications, and in a number of anthologies.

In 1989 Ed was awarded the Lyndhurst Prize, a sustaining grant that supported his work through 1991 and facilitated even deeper exploration of the rest of the answer to the question of the source of a poem. Poets indeed must stop, look, and listen. But then they must find, tap, and pour out the sparkling, thirst-quenching words that serve to refresh the minds and souls of the rest of us. Ed's exploring was stilled, his voice silenced, in 1992 when he died of complications of endocarditis, a treatable disease that had gone untreated because he had no health insurance and no money to pay for care.

–William R. MacKaye

Ed Cox and William R. MacKaye, a writer and editor, were friends for more than twenty years and had many conversations about the structure and content of Part of.

The Dream of a Companion

1. Beginnings

I have not been here long: this wind, these windows,
this way. I see you, yet unmet, as you walk
on the other side of a canal, across the street,
stare skyward from the rising escalator trail.

You are the one I imagine with me in the rain,
beside me in the sweat of the thirsting June light.

You are the dream of a companion. You name
the dream that keeps me going amidst crowds,
when the phone rings once only and not again.

2. From Then

From then—remembered, sheltered—you recall
there was a boy, a stranger, taller than you,
who waved, beckoned with both hands above.

Shutter of dream? Did it occur in the past?
Was it a fall from the sky? Fearful as mud
beneath racing toward your grip on height?

The pack of dogs chases you. An old man's face
distorts the curved mirror flight. You swing
higher and call out, finally, a four letter word
at the night ahead, the scattering of stars.

June 3, 1992